Embracing the Silence:

A Journey Through Autism, Loss, and Acceptance

Dedication

To my son, who teaches me every day that love needs no words.

And to all the parents and caregivers on this journey,

may you find strength in the silence and hope in the unexpected.

Copyright Page

Embracing the Silence: A Mother's Journey Through Autism and Acceptance

Copyright © 2024 by Dr. Lissarette Nisnevich

All rights reserved.

No part of this book may be reproduced, distributed, or transmitted in any form or by any means, including photocopying, recording, or other electronic or mechanical methods, without the prior written permission of the author, except in the case of brief quotations embodied in critical reviews and certain other non-commercial uses permitted by copyright law. For permission requests, please contact the author at the email below.

This book is a work of creative non-fiction. The events are portrayed to the best of the author's memory, though some names and identifying details have been changed to protect the privacy of individuals.

Self-published by Dr. Lissarette Nisnevich

ISBN: 978-1-7366439-2-1

Printed in the United States of America

For inquiries, contact:
info@lissarette.com
www.lissarette.com

Cover Design by [Insert Designer's Name, if applicable]

First Edition: April, 1st 2025

Disclaimer: The information provided in this book is based on personal experiences and should not be considered professional medical, psychological, or therapeutic advice. Always consult a professional when dealing with specific medical or emotional issues.

Table of Contents

- Dedication..i
  - To My Son and Those on This Journey
- Prologue 1
  - Finding Hope in the Silence

1. Shock & Denial 4
   - Story: When the World Changed................5
   - Poem: Silent Shifts...................................14

2. Pain & Guilt 16
   - Story: Carrying the Weight 17
   - Poem: Echoes of Doubt............................24

3. Anger & Bargaining 27
   - Story: What Could I Give? 28
   - Poem: Bargaining with God.....................35

4. Depression 38
   - Story: Falling Apart 39
   - Poem: The Weight of It All 46

5. The Upward Turn 49
   - Story: Finding Clarity 50
   - Poem: The Moment That Mattered 57

6. Reconstruction & Working Through 60
   - Story: Rebuilding Our Lives 61
   - Poem: Rebuilding Us 66

7. Acceptance & Hope 68
   - Story: A New Kind of Love 69
   - Poem: Different, Not Less 74

- Epilogue 78
   - A New Kind of Love
- Resources for Parents and Families 81
   - Autism support organizations, books, podcasts, and local resources 81

Disclaimer

This book is designed to be read in different ways, allowing you to experience it based on what resonates most with you:

1. The Poems: If you prefer to focus on the emotional aspect of the journey, you can read the poems in each chapter. These verses capture the raw feelings of each stage and allow you to feel the intensity of the experience in a more abstract way.

2. The Story: For those looking to follow the narrative of my personal journey, read the stories in each chapter. This will give you a more detailed and practical understanding of the ups and downs, the struggles, and the moments of hope.

3. Both: To get the full experience, read both the poems and the stories. Together, they offer a complete picture, blending emotional depth with the real-world challenges and triumphs that come with raising a neurodiverse child.

Whichever way you choose to read, I hope this book brings you comfort, understanding, and hope.

Prologue

Life rarely goes as planned. For years, I had pictured a future for my son filled with laughter, milestones, and the kind of carefree childhood I had once known. I built an entire life around those expectations—a business, a community, a vision of who we'd become. But sometimes, life shifts in ways that shake you to your core.

The pandemic of 2020 didn't just unravel the world outside—it forced me to confront the unraveling happening within my own home. My beautiful, joyful son began to change. It wasn't immediate. At first, it was the little things—the quiet retreat from his peers, the way he clung to the sounds of Latin American lullabies, his bright, babbling words disappearing into silence.

The isolation of the lockdown mirrored the growing isolation within our lives. What began as confusion quickly morphed into something much more difficult to name—a strange, gnawing fear that the future I had imagined for my son would never be. I denied it at first, telling myself he was simply going through a phase. But soon, I couldn't deny what was unfolding before me.

This book is about the seven stages of grief that I went through as I came to terms with my son's autism. It's about heartbreak, about the anger and despair that threatened to consume me, and ultimately, about acceptance and hope. It's a journey I didn't ask to take, but one that transformed me in ways I never expected.

As you read, you'll walk with me through the darkest corners of fear, guilt, and pain. You'll see how I wrestled with denial, how I fought for answers, and how I slowly, painfully, learned to let go of the life I thought we'd live. But you'll also see the beauty that emerged—the ways my son taught me to love without condition, to listen without speaking, and to embrace the life that is.

Because in the end, it wasn't about him changing to fit the world—it was about me learning to accept the world as he experiences it. This is our story of love, resilience, and the unwavering bond that holds us together as we climb a mountain we once thought impossible to scale. Together, we are moving it, one step at a time.

Stage 1 "Shock & Denial"

Chapter 1: When the World Changed

During the pandemic of 2020, when the world was unraveling in chaos, I sensed something else was wrong. Not just with the news headlines or the fear in people's voices, but with my beautiful, healthy, and joyful toddler. He was changing before my eyes, and it was happening in a way that I couldn't fully understand.

At first, I thought it was just the lockdowns, the isolation, the strange new reality that we were living in. But it wasn't. It was something deeper—something personal and far more unsettling. My son had started to isolate himself from the other children, playing alone in the corner, leaning against the speaker that played Latin American children's songs by Marta Gómez. Her voice became his refuge, the only constant in a world that was slipping further away from him. To this day, it's the music he wants to hear before drifting off to sleep.

But that wasn't the only change. Slowly, the words and phrases he had once said so eagerly began to disappear. His joyful babble was replaced by silence—a silence that felt like an absence of the expressive language we had always shared. My once lively, engaged boy was retreating into himself, becoming someone I no longer knew how to reach. He was slipping into a world I couldn't follow him into, and it terrified me.

What terrified me more, though, was the silence around us. Everyone who should have noticed, everyone who should have said something, remained quiet. Perhaps they were afraid of offending me, or maybe they didn't want to overstep. Maybe they were as confused as I was. But no one spoke up, and I was left to carry the weight of this confusion on my own.

My son was my world—my reason for everything I was building. After opening the daycare where he spent his early years, surrounded by a close-knit group of families who felt like friends, I was now in the process of building a preschool. I had a vision of creating a community, much like the one I'd grown up in back on the island, where children would grow up together, supported by familiar faces. I wanted my son to have that, to feel a sense of identity and belonging that would shape him into someone strong, confident, and loved.

But as my son drifted further away, that dream started to feel like a lie. The world I had built for us began to fall apart. The closest anyone came to addressing what was happening was a teacher who eventually had to be fired—not for pointing out my son's differences, but because she was simply terrible at her job. Still, her comments echoed in my mind. Yet, I remained in denial.

Shock and denial don't even begin to describe the mental acrobatics I performed every time my son exhibited what I knew—deep down—were clear red flags. I made excuses for every one of them. I justified every behavior, convinced myself that I knew better. After all, I was his mother. People would ask, "What does your gut tell you?" But my gut had been screaming for so long that it had turned into a dull, empty ache.

I watched helplessly as my son distanced himself from the other children. But then there was Ella. Ella never gave up on him. She saw beyond his silence, beyond his quirks, and kept inviting him to play, including him in her world. She was patient, kind, and incredibly empathetic. For that, I will forever be grateful. Eventually, Paige joined them, and together they became a regular part of my son's day. They encouraged him, gave him little tasks, and tried to pull him out of his shell in ways I couldn't. It was both heartwarming and heartbreaking to watch. They were doing for my son what I, his mother, couldn't seem to do. And slowly, it worked—little by little, they became his anchors in a sea of uncertainty.

It wasn't until a colleague from Early Intervention urged me, again and again, that I finally scheduled an evaluation. She convinced me that there was nothing to lose, but deep down, I was terrified of what I might find. The day I scheduled the evaluation felt like an admission of defeat—a silent acknowledgment that my son's differences weren't just a phase, weren't something I could fix with love, patience, or time. I arranged for a private speech evaluation because his language delay was my biggest concern at the time.

When the speech therapist confirmed his delay and offered virtual services, I felt a wave of frustration. Virtual therapy—for a toddler? It felt useless, and after two sessions, I discontinued it. The world was crumbling, protests were raging in the streets, and the pandemic had everyone on edge. How could virtual therapy possibly help my son when he needed so much more than a screen could provide?

The stress was overwhelming. My husband and I fought constantly. We argued about everything—the evaluations, our son's behavior, what it looked like versus what it could be. We were clashing at a time when we needed each other most. Instead of finding support, we found isolation. Instead of empathy, we found judgment. The community I had worked so hard to build seemed indifferent to our struggle. The families I had poured my heart into couldn't spare a moment to understand what we were going through.

That's when fear set in. For the first time in my life, I felt powerless. I had always been able to fix things, to solve problems, to make things right. But this? This was beyond me. My son needed help, and I couldn't give it to him. The pandemic made everything worse—no speech therapists could see him in person, evaluation centers were either closed or backlogged. I felt trapped, helpless, and desperate.

When we finally managed to get an appointment, it was a nightmare. Six hours of evaluations, followed by a report filled with "nevers"—a long, painful list of things they said my son would never do. They handed me the "Would Never" list, a document I hated with every fiber of my being. My son would never do this, never do that. I felt crushed under the weight of those words. They weren't just predictions; they felt like sentences handed down from some cruel, indifferent authority.

I cried the entire way home, mourning the future I thought we had lost. I couldn't see a way forward. Everything felt hopeless. The future I had imagined—where my son would thrive in a world I had meticulously built for him—was slipping through my fingers. And I was powerless to stop it.

Yet, through all of this, there was one constant: the love and support of Ella and Paige. They were there for him when I couldn't be. They saw him in ways that even I, his mother, struggled to. While I wished I could say the same for Paige's parents—who were a nightmare to deal with—I will always remember the way their daughter cared for my son when he needed it most. Ella's family, however, remains an example of the kind of compassion I wish the world could show us:

kindness, respect, and a genuine understanding of our journey.

In the end, it wasn't the evaluations, the diagnoses, or even the "Would Never" list that mattered. It was the love, the patience, and the small moments of connection that got us through. Those were the moments I held onto, the moments that reminded me that, no matter how hard it was, my son was still here. He was still mine. And together, we would find our way.

Stage 1 Poem: Silent Shifts

In the year the world stood still,
I watched you change, against my will.
The laughter once so bright and clear,
Began to fade, then disappear.

You leaned against the music's hum,
A corner where you'd quietly come,
While Marta's voice would softly play,
A world that slowly slipped away.

Your words, like whispers in the night,
Took flight on wings, out of my sight.
What once was joy, was now retreat,
A silence in your tiny feet.

And all around, the world was mute,
As if afraid to speak the truth.
Their eyes would dart, their voices still,
Unsure if love could break this chill.

But I could see the growing space,
A gulf within your sweet, young face.
I searched for answers, sought a guide,
Yet grief and doubt were close beside.

I begged for signs, for hands to hold,
But only silence, distant, cold.
Still, Ella stayed, her gentle heart,
A thread that kept you from the dark.

Through every tear, through every fight,
I held you close with all my might.
And though the world refused to see,
You were still everything to me.

So now, we walk this winding way,
With songs to guide us day by day.
No words to tell what's lost, what's found,
But in this love, we still are bound.

For though you turn from where you stood,
I know your heart, I know you're good.
And in the quiet, in the space,
I'll find my son, I'll find my place.

Stage 2 "Pain & Guilt"

Chapter 2: Carrying the Weight

The evaluation brought no relief. I had hoped that the paper—this official diagnosis—would offer some clarity, some sense of direction. I thought it would be a guide, a path forward. But instead, it felt like a slap in the face. It was a harsh confirmation of my worst fears and the beginning of a journey I didn't know how to take. Rather than giving me answers, it left me with more confusion, more despair.

The world outside continued to burn with chaos. Protests filled the streets. The pandemic raged on, isolating everyone in their homes. But inside, my world was engulfed in a different kind of fire—one I couldn't escape. It was a slow, smoldering grief, growing heavier with each passing day. I wanted to make the right decision for my son, to understand why this was happening to us, but I was drowning in the enormity of it all.

I was pursuing a graduate degree to help families like mine, to guide them through their challenges. And now, here I was, unable to help my own family. How had we ended up here, in this dark, lonely place? I felt like a fraud, a mother who should know better but didn't. My professional knowledge suddenly felt hollow, useless in the face of my personal pain.

I had left my job to open a daycare, believing that the early years of development were crucial, that I could create a nurturing environment for children, including my own. But now, I wondered if it had all been in vain. Was I defective? Had my genes caused this? Autism is genetic, after all. My mind spiraled down endless corridors of guilt, questioning everything. What had I done wrong? Could I have prevented this?

My husband and I had decided to refuse genetic testing, fearing it would only deepen the divide between us. We needed unity, but we struggled to find it. My trauma response had always been to flee when things got hard, and I found myself mentally running. I would pack bags in my head, mentally checking the renewal status of my green cards from Asia. I imagined leaving everything behind, disappearing, escaping the madness that consumed me. I wasn't acting like myself, and I knew it. Outside, the world was burning with its own chaos, and inside, I was burning with mine.

Locked inside our home, we fought, grieved, and faced despair. One cold evening, I remember sitting in the backyard, staring at nothing despite the freezing temperatures. My husband found me there, shivering. He wrapped me in a blanket and urged me to come inside, but I remained still, frozen by the weight of it all. The evaluation report sat beside me, a constant reminder of everything I didn't want to accept.

"Can you believe this?" I fumed, my voice shaking. "How can they be so sure? How can they already decide what he will or won't do?" My anger was palpable, boiling over in the bitter night air. The evaluators had reduced my son to a list of limitations, focusing only on the things that confirmed their biases. They didn't see him for who he really was. They didn't see his brilliance, his potential.

"He can count to a thousand," I muttered, trying to find some solace in that fact. "He organizes numbers in ways I can't even understand." I was clinging to the parts of him that defied their bleak diagnosis. My husband, however, remained silent, his face stoic. He believed I was in denial, that this was our son's fate, and that we needed to come to terms with it.

But I had never, in my entire existence, accepted something I didn't believe I deserved. And I wasn't going to start now. This was my son. I refused to let anyone, even the experts, define what he could or couldn't do.

That night, tears carried me back to sleep, but I woke up only a few hours later, overwhelmed by the crushing reality of our situation. It wasn't just the diagnosis weighing on me—it was everything. I found myself chasing after payments from families for months, juggling endless Department of Health visits, and battling a constant storm of anxiety. Everything was too much. I couldn't continue, though deep down, I knew the truth—I didn't want to. My concern for my son had eclipsed everything else. How could I care about the mundane worries of running a business when my son's future was hanging in the balance?
I felt like I was failing at everything. My business, my family, my role as a mother. The daycare, which had once been my dream, now

felt like a battleground. Every day, I found myself comparing my son to the other children. What could they do that he couldn't? I fixated on every difference, every delay. His teachers urged me to focus on his strengths—something I had told countless parents myself—but I couldn't take my own advice. I was too consumed by guilt, too weighed down by the idea that I had somehow failed him.

The days stretched on, long and arduous. Every morning, I called therapists, desperately sending emails that went unanswered. It felt like I was shouting into a void, begging for help that never came. What was hope when I couldn't see the light at the end of the tunnel?

The guilt gnawed at me constantly. If my genes weren't to blame, then maybe it was my husband's. I began to harbor unspoken accusations, lingering doubts about who was responsible. Had we done this to our son? Why was this happening to him? Why did he have to pay the price for something we couldn't even understand?

I had always been the problem solver, the one who could find a way out of any situation. But here, I was lost. There was no solution, no quick fix. Autism wasn't something I could fight. It wasn't an illness with a cure. It was a reality I couldn't change, and that helplessness consumed me.

Stage 2 Poem "Echoes of Doubt"

In the wake of the diagnosis,
I sought answers in sterile white,
But clarity remained elusive,
A shadow in the flickering light.

The world outside was raging,
While inside, I was aflame,
Struggling with the dark confusion,
Grappling with a hollowed name.

I left behind the safety net,
Built dreams from threads of hope,
Yet in the quiet corners of doubt,
I struggled, slipped, and choked.

Was it my fault? My genes to blame?
The question tore through every seam,
The fire within, a burning shame,

Consuming more than it redeems.

In the cold, I sat in frozen still,
The world's chill a distant hum,
Lost in the papers of false will,
Grieving for the battles won.

Silent screams of unspoken fears,
Tears that fell like bitter rain,
As I blamed what couldn't be explained,
And endured the weight of guilt and pain.

Yet in the darkness, glimmers faint,
A whisper of hope, a fragile spark,
Through every sleepless, weary night,
A plea to mend a broken heart.

For though the road was hard and long,
And doubts cast shadows deep and wide,
I sought to find where I belonged,
With love as my unyielding guide.

In the echoes of my silent grief,
I learned to see a glimmered chance,

Lissarette Nisnevich

To face the doubts and find relief,
In the strength of a hopeful stance.

Stage 3: Anger and Bargaining

Chapter 3: What Could I Give?

What does a parent do when their child is in need? If they need a kidney, you give them yours. If they need blood, you offer it without hesitation. Sleepless nights by a hospital bed, bone marrow transplants—there is nothing a parent wouldn't do to ensure their child gets the life they deserve. And I was ready. Like the giving tree, I was willing to offer every part of myself for my son to thrive.

But what could I possibly give to make his autism disappear? What could I sacrifice to make him just like the other kids?

The world I had built for us—this carefully constructed life—began to fall apart. People stopped calling for playdates. The friends I once cherished, the parents who had praised the community I'd created, now whispered behind my back. They texted one another about my son, exchanging their judgments in secret. Some were kind enough—or cruel enough—to share screenshots with me, revealing who was two-faced and who wasn't. But knowing didn't make it hurt any less.

Then came the birthday party. The one I didn't even know about until the children mentioned it. My staff filled in the details—every single child from our class, along with their caregivers, had been invited. Everyone except my son. It wasn't the party that mattered to me; social events had never been high on my list of priorities. But this? This exclusion felt personal, deliberate.

I reached out to the mother, not to demand an invitation, but to ask why. What was it about my boy that made him unworthy of their gathering? I had gone out of my way for this woman—offered her discounts, accommodated her needs when no one else would. And yet, she excluded my son. Her excuse? COVID restrictions. Conveniently, these restrictions seemed to apply only to my son, the autistic child, while everyone else was somehow exempt.

I wanted to scream. I wanted to tell her how her actions had deepened the wound I was already struggling to heal. But I said nothing. Because women like me, women with my background, aren't allowed to grieve openly. We're not allowed to confront or challenge. We're expected to take the exclusion in stride, to swallow the pain and keep moving, as if it's our place to remain silent.

But that day, I made a decision. I didn't need people like her. My son didn't need to be at a party where he wasn't wanted. The anger I felt, however, lingered, burrowing deep inside me.

It hasn't left me since. I hope that mother finds peace, that her child—whom I helped raise alongside my own—never feels the sting of rejection that my son endured. And I hope no other parent ever has to carry the same anger, an anger born from a grief so deep that the selfish, cruel people around us could never understand.

And then there was the anger at home—directed at my husband. Every day, we fought. Over nothing. Over everything. He couldn't understand the depth of my pain, and I resented him for it. I resented him for not feeling it as intensely as I did, for not being consumed by it the way I was. As we clashed, the anger inside me grew, spiraling into darker and darker places.

I prayed. Desperate, relentless prayers. I begged God to take me instead. I prayed for cancer, for pain, for death—anything, so long as my son could live a happy, fulfilling life. I pleaded with God to punish me, to make me suffer instead. Life had already been a gauntlet of abuse and resilience. I had walked through fire before, and I was ready to do it again, if it meant my son could experience the joys of childhood like all the other kids.

Every night, I found myself on my knees, crying out to the heavens. And every chance I got, I stepped into random churches, lighting candles, making promises, offering whatever I had. I bargained with God, told Him I'd give up everything—every ounce of comfort, every dollar we had. I would live in poverty, suffer in silence, if only my son could speak. If only he could smile at me the way other children smile at their mothers. If only he could look me in the eye and say the word that felt so far out of reach: "Mama".

The weight of that absence crushed me. I would do anything to have the child he was becoming before it all changed. Before the word "autism" became this heavy, unspoken thing that clung to every corner of our lives. This wasn't the life I had imagined for him, for us. And it was so much harder than I had ever allowed myself to admit.

Yet, through all the praying, all the bargaining, I couldn't ignore the truth staring me in the face. My son was still here. He was still "him". But I couldn't see it. I couldn't see past what I wanted for him, past what the world expected him to be. And that broke me even more. I hated myself for not being able to love him exactly as he was. I hated myself for clinging so desperately to the child I thought he should be, instead of embracing the child who was right in front of me.

Every day felt like a battle between what I was losing and what I had in front of me. And that battle was bleeding into everything. I couldn't keep pretending that this pain wasn't eating me alive. The anger I felt wasn't just with my husband, with the world, or with God—it was with myself. I had built my life on being strong, resilient, a woman who could survive anything. But here I was, crumbling under the weight of my son's difference.

I was losing sight of the beauty in who he was becoming, blinded by the anger and grief of what he might never be. And in that blindness, I realized I was losing him. I was letting my anger push me further from him, and that realization broke me in ways I wasn't ready to confront.

There was no bargaining that could change who he was, no prayer that could erase his autism. And yet, in my heart, I couldn't stop asking. I couldn't stop hoping for a miracle I knew would never come. I wanted to fix this, to make everything better. But this wasn't something I could fix. And that reality—that powerlessness—was a weight I wasn't sure I could carry.

Stage 3 Poem "Bargaining with God"

I'm angry at him,
angry at the way we fight—
over nothing, over everything,
as if the air between us is sharp enough
to slice through our love,
as if he can't see
the storm that lives in me.

I pray to a God
who I'm not sure is listening.
Take me instead,
I beg,
give me cancer, give me pain,
give me death
if you'll only give my son
the life I've imagined for him.

Let him speak, let him smile,

Lissarette Nisnevich

let him look into my eyes
and say, "Mama".
I would trade my every breath
to hear that word.
I would live in rags,
forsake every comfort,
if he could just be
the child I dreamed,
the child I was promised.

But promises break
like fragile bones
under the weight of reality.
Every church becomes an altar
for my desperation,
knees pressed into cold stone,
hands clasped so tight,
they ache with my pleas.
I offer everything I have,
but nothing changes.

The silence stretches on,
and I am still here,

wrestling with a love
that doesn't look like I thought it would.

I'm angry at him,
angry at myself—
for not being able to see
the beauty in what is,
for clinging so tightly
to what will never be.
I'm losing him,
I know,
caught in the grief of what I wanted
instead of the gift
of who he already is.

And in my blindness,
I bargain with God,
but all I'm really asking
is for peace
with this version of my son
that I can't stop grieving.

Stage 4: Depression

Chapter 4: Falling Apart

As my world—my precious son's world—came crashing down around me, I felt completely powerless. The action-packed, take-charge woman I had always been was suddenly paralyzed. And as everything crumbled, new chaos seemed to find its way to us, as if drawn to our vulnerability.

It was our wedding anniversary. A day my husband had hoped would lift my spirits, a day when he tried so hard to make me smile. My therapist, meanwhile, worked tirelessly to keep me off medication, sensing that I was on the edge. And then, just when I thought things couldn't get worse, The Jokers struck again.

The Jokers—a family who paraded around like they were compassionate and kind, when in reality, they were anything but. Racist, discriminatory, and entitled, they had caused me endless stress. Yet, I tolerated them because their daughter, Paige, was sweet to my son. That, at least, mattered to me.

That day is forever burned into my memory. Mr. Joker brought his sick, medicated son to my center, despite knowing the rules. He demanded to see me, entitled as ever, but I was too far gone to care. Normally, I would have stormed out there to confront him, but my husband stepped in instead. We all watched from inside as Mr. Joker screamed and threatened him—threatened death, violence, and even a lawsuit—all while holding his one-year-old son in his arms. It played out like some twisted show, a spectacle of his rage and entitlement.

But I didn't care. I didn't have the energy to react. The anger, the frustration—it had all been swallowed by something far darker. I was numb. I couldn't bring myself to feel anything beyond the sadness that weighed me down like a lead blanket.

I stopped eating. My staff would slip plates of food into my office, trying to coax me with jokes, with love, hoping something would get through to me. But I could barely bring myself to touch the food. I had no appetite—not for food, not for life. I stopped calling therapists, stopped trying to find help. It was a battle just to get out of bed in the mornings. Every small task felt insurmountable, and every day felt like an endless stretch of nothingness.

The gossip never stopped. Screenshots of parents' conversations kept flooding in— comments about how distant I had become, speculations about my marriage, about how obvious it was that we were headed for divorce.

I didn't care. I had always cared too much about what others thought of me, but now? Now, I felt nothing. Even my husband, who had never been one to care about what others said, knew something was terribly wrong when I stopped reacting to the whispers.

The business I had worked so hard to build now felt like an enemy. Between the ungrateful clients and the surprise inspections from the state, I began to see that I had been giving my attention to all the wrong things. I started pulling my son out of class early, taking him for long walks in nature, just the two of us. Those were the only moments when the suffocating sadness lifted, even if just a little. In those moments, I could breathe again.

As I walked with my son, I found myself observing other parents—parents with neurotypical, healthy children, parents who seemed indifferent to the gifts they had been given. And yes, I judged them. I judged them the same way they had judged me, the way they whispered about my son. They thought they knew my life, but they didn't. They had no idea. I pitied their children. What wouldn't I give to have my son talk my ear off about his day, to see him express himself like those other kids? One day, a father left his sick child at our doorstep—a defenseless toddler, abandoned during a pandemic, when we had explicitly told him not to bring the child for everyone's safety. He just walked away. We all watched the video in disbelief, another act of cruelty, another reminder of the world's indifference.

I started to wonder: Did I care too much? Was that my problem? Here I was, falling apart because my son wouldn't speak, wouldn't engage with the world. Meanwhile, other parents seemed to treat their children like props, accessories to their lives.

I stopped trying to bridge the gap between my son and the other kids. I no longer offered rewards to the children if they played with him, no longer asked the staff to integrate him into activities. I stopped answering emails. I stopped writing the blogs that used to bring me joy. There was no joy left. What was the point? What joy could there possibly be when the future looked so bleak?

The worst part wasn't even the sadness—it was the isolation. I couldn't talk to anyone about how I really felt. I had always been the strong, independent woman, the one who could handle anything, the one who others looked up to. But now, I was barely holding it together. And I knew, deep down, that people were waiting for me to fail. Like vultures, they circled, waiting for my downfall. Clients, friends, even family. They were waiting to see me fall apart.

And for the first time in my life, I was ready to let them. I was ready to give up. Autism wasn't something I could fight. It wasn't an illness with a cure, wasn't something that could be fixed. It was a reality I had to live with, a reality that felt impossibly heavy. It felt like God didn't want my son to experience the joy that other children took for granted, and that thought—more than anything else—broke me.

I wanted to scream at the world. I wanted to collapse under the weight of it all, to disappear into the darkness that had crept into my bones. I didn't know who I was anymore, and worse, I didn't know how to find my way back.

Stage 4 Poem "The Weight of It All"

I used to be strong—
the kind of woman who could carry
the weight of the world
on my shoulders,
but now,
it's too heavy.

The walls I built,
brick by resilient brick,
are crumbling.
I stand in the ruins,
watching my son's world collapse,
powerless to save him,
powerless to save myself.

I prayed once—
for miracles, for mercy,
for a cure that would never come.
Now I barely speak,
my voice swallowed by the silence
that surrounds us.

I watch him,
wondering what joy feels like
for a child who doesn't speak.
I wonder what I did wrong,
why God turned His face away,
why my boy can't know the world
as they do—
those children whose parents
seem to care so little.

I stopped trying,
stopped pretending that I could fix it.
The vultures can circle;
let them.
I'm ready to be picked apart,
to be swallowed by the darkness
that has crept into my bones.

Lissarette Nisnevich

This isn't something I can fight,
and I'm tired.
Autism is a battle with no end,
and I am a soldier
who's lost her way.
I watch him,
and I wonder—
what would it feel like
to hear him call me "Mama",
to see him live a life
without this weight
we both carry?

Stage 5: The Upward Turn

Chapter 5: Finding Clarity

I couldn't figure out what really mattered anymore. It felt like everything was screaming for my attention all at once, but deep down, I knew the truth. My son needed all of me—right now. Not the pieces of me that were left after managing a business or the scraps I had leftover after worrying about everyone else's expectations.

I had built a successful business, treating it like an extension of our family. Every decision I made, every promise I gave to the families who trusted me, came from a place of genuine belief. I poured my heart into that business, believing it was just as important as the home I was building for my son. But the cracks started to show when I realized that love and loyalty weren't being returned. People were quick to take but slow to give back.

Then, we took a trip to Florida—a place we had always dreamed of moving to in the future. It was supposed to be a decade away, but we found ourselves there, sooner than expected, searching for something we couldn't quite name. And on that trip, it was as if a weight was lifted off my shoulders. The heavy backpack of burdens I'd been carrying suddenly felt lighter. For the first time in what felt like forever, the fog began to clear.

Two days after we arrived, my son spoke. Just a few single words, but they were monumental to me. We stayed by the beach, playing in the sand every day. And though I was still working, I could see things from a new perspective. Everything started to fall into place. What truly mattered became so clear.

Our family began to reconnect in ways we hadn't in a long time. My husband and I had uninterrupted time to talk about our future, to talk about what was important. And during one of those long walks by the water, he told me something that I hadn't realized I needed to hear.

"I'll do anything," he said, his voice soft but sure. "For you, for our son—whatever it takes."

And I believed him. Through everything, he had been by my side. Even when I was breaking, when I felt like I had nothing left, he never wavered. He juggled his own demanding job while still believing in me—believing in us. He never stopped believing in what I could do, in the things I was yet to do.

Then, he asked me a question that changed everything.

"Do you want to quit? I can support us. You can be with him."

My heart skipped a beat. I felt it physically, that moment when the weight of what I had been carrying shifted inside me. For so long, I had been holding onto this business, convinced that it was my purpose, that it was worth the endless sacrifices. But in that moment, I realized the truth. I didn't need this business. My son needed me. The children who had grown up with him, the families who had once felt like our family—they were all gone. The people who remained had no real connection to me, no loyalty.

The more I grew this business, the more it demanded of my mental health. The further it pulled me from my son. And it became clear that the business was asking me to choose it over him. And there was no way in hell I was going to do that.

So, when my husband offered to support us, I accepted. The decision wasn't just about walking away from the business—it was about reclaiming my life. If the world didn't want to make space for my son, then I would. If nobody wanted to see him, to accept him, then I would see him. I would learn how to help him thrive, even if it wasn't perfect. It would be done with love, and it would be done right. He wouldn't have to question whether he was wanted or loved, because I would make sure he knew, every single day, that he was more than enough.

We spent our days watching the sunset, letting the waves soothe us. And then, something extraordinary happened. One evening, as my husband and I sat quietly by the water, my son walked up to us. He looked us both in the eye—something I had almost stopped hoping for—and he said, "I love you."

For a moment, I couldn't breathe. My husband and I just stared at each other, speechless. In that simple sentence, all the doubt, all the fear, all the pain melted away. We knew, without a shadow of a doubt, that we had made the right decision.

Nothing else mattered. Not the business, not the judgment of others, not the expectations the world had placed on us. What mattered was right there with us, in the sand, in the fading light of the sunset, in those three precious words our son had just spoken.

And for the first time in a long while, I felt peace. Real peace. The kind that comes when you stop fighting against what life is asking of you and instead, surrender to the beauty of what's in front of you.

I realized that I didn't need to hold onto the old dreams I had built. They weren't worth sacrificing my son's well-being, or my own. And

Lissarette Nisnevich

as I stood on that beach, I felt a quiet certainty that the future, however uncertain, was filled with hope.

Stage 5 Poem "The Moment That Mattered"

I carried the weight of the world,
bricks stacked high on my back,
a fortress built around a life
that no longer felt like mine.
But in the sand, under the sun,
the walls began to crumble.

What truly matters?
I asked the sea,
the waves whispering answers
I already knew.

My son spoke—
a single word,
small,

but heavy with hope.
And suddenly, the fog lifted.

I had built an empire,
but it cost me more than I could pay.
The families were gone,
the laughter faded,
and I was left with strangers
in a place that asked too much.

But in that quiet moment,
by the shore,
we found ourselves again.
My husband's hand in mine,
his voice soft, "I can carry us."
And for the first time, I let go.
The world didn't need my son—
so I would be his world.
I would show him love,
in every step,
every sunrise,
every wave that kissed the shore.

And then he spoke,
the words I had longed for:
"I love you."
The moment that mattered,
etched in the sand,
forever in our hearts.

In that moment, we knew—
we had found what truly mattered.

Stage 6: "Reconstruction and Working Through"

Chapter 6: Rebuilding Our Lives

We rewrote the entire script of our lives. All the plans we had meticulously laid out for the future—opening an elementary school, expanding it through high school, taking over the entire building—suddenly felt irrelevant. The dreams we had for our business were no longer our priority. Instead, we began to craft a new plan—one that would center around my son.

We started working on a homeschooling plan, something that would nurture his strengths and allow him to grow in a world that made sense for him. No longer would I hide him away out of fear. Fear of bullying, fear of the stares in public places, fear of judgment. That fear had controlled me for too long. Now, I was showing up for him, unapologetically. When people looked at him differently, when they tried to discriminate against him, I didn't shrink away. I simply let them know he was autistic, as if it were the most natural thing in the world. Because it was. This was who he was, and there was nothing to hide.

I stayed close to him, making sure he was treated with the kindness and respect he deserved, but also allowing him the space to be himself. Through me, he felt empowered to embrace his differences. And through him, I was learning what it meant to truly be free.

I began to get comfortable with being uncomfortable. I stopped trying to make the world conform to my expectations. Instead, I started meeting my son where he was. We bought a beautiful place by the beach, and we began mapping out what our future would look like once we moved there.

At the same time, I started making decisions about the business that had once consumed my life. I had been holding onto it out of habit, out of fear of letting go, but I realized it no longer served us. I started planning how to transition out, to either close it down or sell it to someone who was more passionate about the journey than I was. And with that decision came a profound sense of relief. I took back control of my personal life, reclaiming the parts of me that I had given away so easily.

I had allowed people far too much access to my life, my struggles, my vulnerability. For what? For validation? For acceptance? I realized I didn't need that anymore. What I needed was my power back. My privacy. My peace.

My husband had transitioned to working remotely, and together, we watched our son bloom. He began using expressive language, little by little, chipping away at the limitations the world had tried to place on him. He started to do things we had been told he would "never" be able to do. Each milestone was a quiet victory. He began to show interest in things outside of his comfort zone, exploring new ideas and stories, stepping beyond the routines that once confined him.

I stopped focusing on what he couldn't do and started celebrating what he could. My son had gifts—gifts that were extraordinary. He had a natural talent for math, an ability to organize numbers and solve problems in ways that left me in awe. If I hadn't been so terrible at math myself, I might have thought about helping him apply to NASA one day.

Life, for the first time in a long time, started to make sense again. There was a rhythm to our days that felt peaceful, grounded. I felt a calm inside me that had been missing for years. The chaos of the past—the anxiety, the sleepless nights, the overwhelming sadness—had begun to fade. And in its place was hope.

I finally felt good. For the first time in two years, I had hope for the future, a future that was different from the one I had imagined but no less meaningful. My son was thriving, in his own way, in his own time. And that was all that mattered.

We had rewritten the narrative. Instead of chasing after the dreams I thought we should have, we were living the life that made sense for us, for our family. And I was no longer afraid of what the world thought. I was no longer chasing the validation of others or trying to meet their expectations.

What mattered was right in front of me—my son, my family, and the quiet, beautiful life we were building together.

Stage 6 Poem "Rebuilding Us"

We rewrote the pages of our lives,
once filled with plans for schools and dreams too big,
now sketched with quiet mornings by the sea,
a new path carved just for him,
and for me.

No more hiding in shadows,
no more shrinking from the world's sharp stares.
I stood tall for him,
his voice found through mine.
Empowered to be,
unafraid to show the world
the beauty they couldn't see.

I watched him bloom,

each word a victory,
each step defying the "never" they had told us.
He explored the world outside his comfort,
and I stopped counting what he couldn't do,
marveling instead at the gifts he held,
the numbers that danced in his brilliant mind.
We traded the noise for the sound of waves,
found peace in the quiet,
and in the space we created,
he grew,
we grew.
Life didn't go as planned,
but now it finally made sense.

And as the sun set over the ocean,
I felt hope bloom inside me,
fragile, yet fierce.
A future reborn,
our story rewritten,
page by page,
with love.

Stage 7: Acceptance & Hope

Chapter 7: A New Kind of Love

My son is autistic, and that is never going to change. It took me time to fully understand that, but once I did, it became clear: he is different, not less. Like Temple Grandin's mother once said, "Different, not less." That phrase had always resonated with me, but it took on a new depth of meaning when I finally let go of trying to change him and started focusing on loving him as he is.

I had spent so long worrying about how to "fix" things, how to make him fit into the world, how to help him be more like the other children. But that wasn't the point. He didn't need to change. I needed to change the way I saw him. My son was living his best life, and instead of investing time and energy into telling him he wasn't enough, I began to show him he was more than enough. I let him know that he was perfect just as he was, and that his future was his to define.

Eventually, it will be up to him to decide what brings him joy, what he wants to pursue. He's a reserved person, unlike me, but I've come to learn that his quietness is part of who he is. He doesn't need to be loud or social to be happy. He loves singing, swimming, and numbers. Those are the things that light him up, and I've made it my mission to connect with him over those shared interests.

I worked on improving my swimming just so I could join him in the pool, so we could splash around together and share that joy. I started introducing him to songs, and with my own love for music, karaoke became our little bonding activity. I'd sing, and he'd watch, captivated. We even started dancing together sometimes, something I never thought we'd do.

It wasn't the "normal" life I'd imagined, but it was ours, and it was beautiful.

I realized that the timeline I had placed on him—the expectations I had for when he should speak, or do certain things—didn't matter anymore. I stopped measuring his progress against anyone else's. I know he'll be fine. He just needs more time. And I've come to understand that just because something works for other children doesn't mean it will work for him. Autism isn't a one-size-fits-all experience. You meet one person with autism, and you've met that person. Each autistic individual is unique, and my son is no exception.

Getting to know him, truly knowing him, has been an incredible gift. It has taught me more about myself than I ever expected. In so many ways, I've had to grow right alongside him. I've learned to stop filling the silence with my own words, to listen more, to be intentional about how I express myself. My son seeks touch constantly, something I was never entirely comfortable with. But I've learned to meet him where he is. I've become more open, more willing to embrace what he needs.

I am no longer afraid. I'm no longer desperate for him to fit in. Those who are meant to love him will love him for exactly who he is. I don't need to force him into a mold that wasn't made for him. The motherhood journey I had imagined isn't the one I'm on, and that's okay. In fact, it's more than okay—it's a different kind of beautiful, a new kind of adventure. I have stopped grieving for the life I thought we would live, and now, I'm excited for the one we're creating.

I used to be embarrassed, not by my son or by the motherhood experience, but by how the world made us feel—how people around us reacted to his differences. I wanted him to feel loved and welcomed, but I realized that's my job as his mother. I am the one who will show him, every day, that he is loved and accepted, no matter what the world says. That's every parent's job. The opinions of others? They no longer have power over me. The world can take a hike. We're doing things our way.

Now, I'm filled with hope. I'm excited for the future, not just for my son but for our entire family. We're going to show the world that not only can this mountain be moved, but that the journey itself can be one of joy, fulfillment, and love. We may not be walking the path I expected, but it's the one we were meant to be on, and I'm grateful for it.

In the end, it wasn't about changing my son. It was about changing how I saw him. And in that shift, I found peace, acceptance, and hope for the future—because it's a future that's filled with love.

Stage 7 Poem "Different, Not Less"

My son is different,
and that's how it's meant to be.
Not broken, not needing to be fixed,
but beautifully, uniquely free.

I used to search for answers,
ways to make him fit the mold,
but now I see the beauty
in the story yet untold.
He loves the water,
so I learned to swim,
and when he sings,
I sing with him.
Together we find joy
in the rhythm of our days,
dancing in the quiet

in our own special ways.

I've learned to listen
to the silence between words,
to speak with meaning,
to let his heart be heard.
The world may judge,
but it's love he'll know,
because I'll show him,
in every way I can,
he is enough, just as he is—
my beautiful, gifted little man.

I no longer grieve the life
I thought we'd live,
instead, I embrace the one we have to give.
This journey is ours,
and it's filled with hope,
with mountains to move
and new ways to cope.

So let the world take a hike,
we'll build our own way,

Lissarette Nisnevich

and find joy and fulfillment
in every single day.

The End…

Of that part of our story :)

Epilogue: A New Kind of Love

If you had told me, years ago, that I would find peace in the life I have now, I wouldn't have believed you. Back then, I was consumed by fear and sadness—grieving the future I thought I had lost for my son. I couldn't see beyond the diagnosis, beyond the silence. But through this journey, I have come to understand something deeply beautiful: my son's life is not less than anyone else's. It's simply different.

In this difference, I've discovered a love that is bigger than words, a patience that I didn't know I had, and a joy that comes from the smallest of moments. I have watched my son grow, not into the child I imagined, but into the person he was always meant to be. And in accepting him for who he is, I have learned to accept myself—my own strengths, my own limitations, and my own place in this unpredictable world.

This journey is not a straight path. There are still days when I feel the weight of uncertainty, days when I wish I could make the world a kinder place for my son, where I wonder what the future will look like. But there are also days when I watch him playing, laughing, or simply being, and I am filled with a quiet gratitude. Not for what we have overcome, but for what we have found.

The grief I felt in the beginning—the sorrow for what I thought we were losing—has transformed into something else. It has become a deep, abiding appreciation for the life we have, for the lessons my son has taught me, and for the love that has grown between us.

This is not the motherhood journey I expected, but it is one I have learned to cherish. I have come to realize that love is not measured by milestones or achievements. It's found in the connection between us—in the way we understand each other, even without words.

For those of you reading this, navigating your own path through a similar journey, I want you to know that you are not alone. Whether you are just beginning, or you've been walking this road for some time, there are resources, communities, and people who can help you, guide you, and remind you that there is hope in even the most difficult moments.

Resources for Parents and Families:

The journey through parenting a neurodiverse child can feel isolating at times, but there is a wealth of support available. Below are some resources that have helped me and countless other families find guidance, comfort, and understanding:

- Autism Speaks
 Website: www.autismspeaks.org
 Autism Speaks offers a wide range of resources for families, from early signs and diagnosis to treatment options and support networks. Their toolkits and educational materials can be invaluable for navigating the early stages of your journey.

- The National Autism Association

Website: www.nationalautismassociation.org

This organization focuses on safety, advocacy, and providing practical resources for families of children with autism. They offer programs for parents and caregivers, as well as information on crisis prevention.

- Autistic Self Advocacy Network (ASAN)
Website: www.autisticadvocacy.org

ASAN is run by and for autistic individuals. They provide a different perspective, focusing on self-advocacy and the rights of people with autism. Their resources can help parents better understand the importance of respecting neurodiversity.

- Books and Podcasts:
- Uniquely Human by Dr. Barry Prizant: This book offers a compassionate look at autism and

emphasizes understanding behaviors as human, rather than symptoms to be "fixed."

- The Autism Podcast: A series of interviews with experts, parents, and advocates that provides practical advice, personal stories, and emotional support.

- *"Thinking in Pictures"*: This Emmy-award winning film tells the incredible story of Temple Grandin, a woman with autism who overcame enormous challenges to become a renowned animal behaviorist and advocate for neurodiverse individuals. It offers a profound look at the importance of recognizing the unique gifts of people with autism.

- Local Support Groups:
Every community has local autism support groups where families can share their experiences, ask questions, and connect with others who understand. Look for listings at community centers, autism advocacy groups, or online forums to find support near you.

A Final Thought:

If you are feeling overwhelmed, scared, or unsure of what comes next, please reach out. You don't have to walk this path alone. The love you have for your child is powerful, and the community you can find will give you strength. Whether it's through these resources or personal connections, you will find your way. And along the journey, you'll discover that the love you share with your child is far more important than the words left unspoken.

As I close this chapter of my life, I am not saying goodbye to the challenges or the emotions that come with being a parent to a neurodiverse child. But I am embracing a new kind of love—a love that doesn't need to be spoken to be felt, a love that isn't tied to expectations, but is as boundless as the journey itself.

Thank you for walking this path with me. I hope you find peace, joy, and above all, the strength to embrace the life that is unfolding before you.

With love,
Dr. Lissarette Nisnevich

www.ingramcontent.com/pod-product-compliance
Lightning Source LLC
Chambersburg PA
CBHW052112200426
43209CB00056B/1566